CODE

St[...]

Alison Hawes • **Jon Stuart**

Contents

OXFORD
UNIVERSITY PRESS

Macro Marvel
(billionaire inventor)

Welcome to Micro World!

Macro Marvel invented Micro World – a micro-sized theme park where you have to shrink to get in.

A computer called *CODE* controls Micro World and all the robots inside – MITEs and BITEs.

A MITE

A BITE

Disaster strikes!

CODE goes wrong on opening day.
CODE wants to shrink the world.

Macro Marvel is trapped inside the park …

Enter Team X!

Four micro agents – *Max, Cat, Ant* and *Tiger* – are sent to rescue Macro Marvel and defeat CODE.

Mini Marvel joins Team X.

Mini Marvel
(Macro's daughter)

In the last book ...

* Max, Cat and Mini looked for the Spider-BITE in the jungle.

* The Spider-BITE released lots of little Spider-BITEs and Max got bitten.

* Cat used her magni-beam to find a cure for Max's bite.

**CODE key
(4 collected)**

You are in the Jungle Trail zone.

3

Before you read

Sound checker

Say the sounds.

oe   **ue**

Sound spotter

Blend the sounds.

g	oe	s

ar	g	ue

t	r	ue

t	u	b	e

Tricky words

many
oh
any

Into the zone

What do you think jungle plants like to feed on?

Hungry Plants

The heroes are in Jungle Trail. Ant looked up jungle plants on his watch.

"There are many hungry plants in the jungle," said Ant.

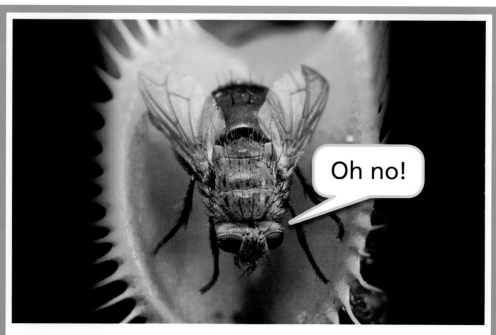

Oh no!

This plant feeds on insects. It snaps up any insect that lands on it!

It's true! Many plants trap insects!

open

closed

insect

This plant is shaped like a tube.

This frog has tumbled into the tube – the plant will feed on it!

This plant feeds on insects too. Any insect that goes too close to it gets stuck like glue!

Don't argue with this sticky plant!

Now you have read ...
Hungry Plants

Take a closer look

How does each plant catch insects?

Thinking time

Why did Ant say, "Don't argue with this sticky plant"?

Can you explain this in your own words?

Before you read

Sound checker
Say the sounds.

oe **ue**

Sound spotter
Blend the sounds.

c	l	ue

r	e	s	c	ue

t	i	p	t	oe

w	o	k	e

Tricky words
many
any
oh

Into the zone

Do you think Max and Ant
will trap the Spider-BITE?

The BITE Trap

Max and Ant set off to find the BITE.

"I've never seen so many sticky plants!" said Ant.
Suddenly, Ant stubbed his toe, tripped and fell onto them!

"Any chance of some help?" Ant shouted to Max.
Max had to use his power mitts to rescue Ant!

Then Max saw a huge spider's web on the side of an old temple. "That's a useful clue!" said Max. "I bet the BITE is in there!"

The Spider-BITE was asleep inside the temple.

"Let's tiptoe up to it and get the CODE key," said Max.

Max and Ant tiptoed closer but the BITE woke up!
"Oh no!" said Ant.

Max and Ant ran, but the BITE pursued them.

"Shrink!" said Max.

"But ..." said Ant.

"Don't argue, Ant!" shouted Max.

Max and Ant ran under the sticky plants.
The BITE fired its web — it stuck like glue to the plants.

The BITE was trapped! Max
and Ant grew and pulled out
the CODE key.
"We're heroes!" Max said.

Now you have read ...
The BITE Trap

Take a closer look

Read the split sentences explaining what happened
to Max and Ant. Can you join the right pieces together
using the word 'so'?

Ant was stuck on
the sticky plants ...

... he knew where
to find the BITE.

Max saw a huge
spider's web ...

so

... the BITE
pursued them.

Max and Ant woke
up the Spider-BITE ...

... Max had to
rescue him.

Thinking time

Look at the pictures and imagine what Max and Ant
are thinking or feeling.